The United States Economy

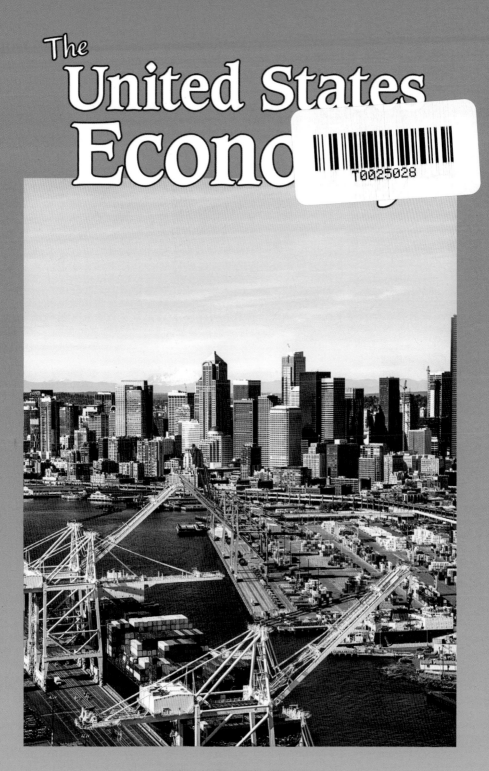

Alex Dalenberg

Consultant

Jennifer M. Lopez, NBCT, M.S.Ed.
Teacher Specialist—History/Social Studies
Office of Curriculum & Instruction
Norfolk Public Schools

Publishing Credits

Rachelle Cracchiolo, M.S.Ed., *Publisher*

Conni Medina, M.A.Ed., *Editor in Chief*

Emily R. Smith, M.A.Ed., *Content Director*

Véronique Bos, *Creative Director*

Robin Erickson, *Art Director*

Michelle Jovin, M.A., *Associate Editor*

Mindy Duits, *Senior Graphic Designer*

Image Credits: p.10 Steve Jurvetson/Flickr; p.11 (top) Yale University Library, Beinecke Rare Book and Manuscript Library; p.11 (bottom) National Museum of American History; p.12 (middle) Library of Congress [LC-USZ62-23640]; p.15 (left) Library of Congress [LC-DIG-hec-26519]; p.15 (right) Library of Congress [LC-DIG-hec-26518]; p.18 Library of Congress [LC-DIG-hec-29174]; pp.18–19 Pixabay; p.19 (bottom) Library of Congress [LC-DIG-ppmsca-49977]; p.20 Everett Historical/Shutterstock; p.21 Library of Congress [LC-DIG-fsa-8d28228]; p.25 (middle) Library of Congress Geography and Map Division [G4872.P3 1881 .W8]; p.25 (bottom right) Library of Congress [LC-USZ62-48614]; p.28 Los Angeles County Department of Public Health; all other images from iStock and/or Shutterstock.

Teacher Created Materials

5301 Oceanus Drive
Huntington Beach, CA 92649-1030
www.tcmpub.com

ISBN 978-0-7439-2316-3

Table of Contents

Our Economy

The United States has one of the largest economies in the world. It is made up of four major **sectors**. These are households, businesses, banks, and the government. You are part of the economy. You live in a household. You buy things from businesses. If you have a bank account, you are part of the banking sector. Lastly, the government provides goods and services for you, such as public schools and sidewalks.

All four sectors work together. Households provide the economy with resources. One of these resources is the money that people who live in households earn. When people want to buy something, they turn to businesses—another part of the economy. People in households and businesses store their money in banks. In return, bankers use this money to **invest** in the economy. Finally, people in the government provide goods and services. The government pays for these things by collecting money. All four sectors depend on each other to thrive. Together, they make up the United States economy.

World Economies

The size of a country's economy is the total of all the goods and services it produces. China has the biggest economy in the world. The United States is second, and India is third.

What Is an Economy?

An *economy* is where things are made, sold, traded, and used. There are many types of economies. States have economies. Countries also have economies. There is even a world economy. This is a sum of all countries' economies.

businesses

banks

government

households

UNITED STATES
FEDERAL RESERVE SYSTEM

Households and Businesses

Households are made up of all the people living together under one roof. This is often a family, but it doesn't have to be. All households have resources. These include land, labor, capital, and **entrepreneurship**. Some people make money by renting their land for others to use. They can also sell things that come from the land. For example, imagine a baker who makes peach pies. The baker can plant peach trees and use the fruit to make pies and earn money.

Households are also made up of people who can work. The work people do is called *labor*. People earn money for their labor. They can use that money to buy things that will help them make more money. These things are called *capital*. For example, imagine the baker needs a new oven and a few new pie pans to keep up with the **demand** their peach pies have caused. The pans and the oven are now part of the baker's capital, since the baker can use those goods to make money.

Goods vs. Services

Goods are physical products. It takes labor to turn natural resources into goods that can be sold. Think about that peach pie. Someone needs to pick the peaches so they can be turned into pies. Then, someone needs to bake the pies. *Services* are work performed for others. The baker provides the service of making pies. A dentist provides the service of filling cavities from eating too many pies.

The fourth resource is entrepreneurship. This involves combining the other three resources—land, labor, and capital—to make money. For example, the baker uses their land to grow peaches. They labor to bake the pies. Finally, they use their capital—the oven and pans—to produce more goods. All these things combine to make the baker an entrepreneur.

Types of Labor

When people go to work, they're selling their labor for money. Some people sell their work by the hour, such as an employee at a bakery. Some workers make a yearly **salary**, such as a dentist. Other workers are paid for each thing they make, such as an artist who sells a painting.

Businesses are the second sector of the economy. Businesses need resources to operate. Those resources come from households. One resource is land, which is owned by people in households. This land might be used for offices, storage, farming, or for other uses. Business owners also need labor and capital. Think about an airline company. Airline owners need airplanes (capital) to provide their service. (The service is flying people from place to place.) The capital belongs to the airline. The company belongs to someone in a household.

Businesses are owned and run by people from households. Sometimes, many people own a company. They may do this by buying stocks. When people buy stocks, they are buying part of a company's ownership. These people are called *shareholders*. Anytime the company makes money, shareholders earn part of the **profits**. On the other hand, when the company loses money, they lose too. This is one more way that sectors of the economy interact.

▲ A shareholder checks how their stocks are performing.

The Stock Market

Companies that want to sell stocks are listed on the stock market. Most companies on the stock market list their stocks on one of two **stock exchanges**. They are the New York Stock Exchange and NASDAQ. Those are the two largest stock exchanges in the world, and both are based in the United States.

Retirement Plans

Many people who own stocks do so through **retirement** funds. One of the most common retirement funds is a 401(k). With 401(k) plans, money is taken out of people's paychecks automatically. Some of that money is then used to buy stocks. When people retire, they can "cash in" their retirement plans. Then, they take the money they invested plus any money that their stocks have earned.

◄ An airplane mechanic provides labor by fixing planes (capital).

People in households and businesses provide entrepreneurship. *Entrepreneurs* are people who use their talents and creativity to make money. This may happen by starting new businesses. Or, they may find ways to combine resources to create new goods and services. Take the bakery owner, for example. They use peaches from the land, labor from the kitchen workers, and the capital of the bakery to make pies. If they can find a better way to combine those resources, they will make more money. Maybe they can find a faster way to make pies. That would allow them to sell more goods. Or maybe they can find a cheaper way to grow peaches. They might use the money they saved from the faster production process to hire more workers or to research new pie recipes. Any of those things would make them an entrepreneur.

The more successful entrepreneurs are, the more they will contribute to the economy. Their households will have more money to buy more things. Their companies will have more money to invest in land, labor, and capital. These investments help people in other households. With growing businesses, there are more jobs available. As more people find work, they too can invest in more things. The cycle goes on and on.

◀ Entrepreneur Salman Khan founded the Khan Academy—a popular online school.

Word Origins

The word *entrepreneur* comes from French. It was first used by Jean-Baptiste Say. Say came up with the word after reading a book by Adam Smith, who was a famous economist.

Self-Made Millionaire

One of the world's most successful entrepreneurs was Madam C. J. Walker. Both of Walker's parents had died by the time she was 7 years old. Walker worked various jobs before starting her own hair-care business. When Walker died in 1919, she had around $800,000. That is more than $12 million today!

Banks and the Government

Banks are the third sector of the United States economy. The banking sector serves people in both households and businesses. Banks give them a place to keep their money. Having money stored in banks is necessary for the economy to succeed. Banks help money move through the economy more easily. This makes the economy more **efficient** by helping the different sectors work together.

Many people in households and businesses put money they earn in banks. This is safer than keeping it at home or carrying it around everywhere. People can feel that their money is safe. In return, bankers can use that money to contribute to the economy. When people put money in banks, it doesn't just sit there. Bankers give that money to people and businesses through **loans**. People with loans have to pay the money back over time. They also have to pay a little extra. This is called *interest*. Banks make money by charging interest on loans. In return, banks pay interest to people who have accounts with the banks.

This system is very important to the flow of the economy. It makes sure that money is always being put to good use. Instead of having money sit untouched, people can spend it. That helps the economy grow.

Wall Street

The banking sector is sometimes called Wall Street. The name comes from an actual street in New York City. Many banks have their main offices nearby. Wall Street is also home to major stock exchanges, where people buy and sell stocks.

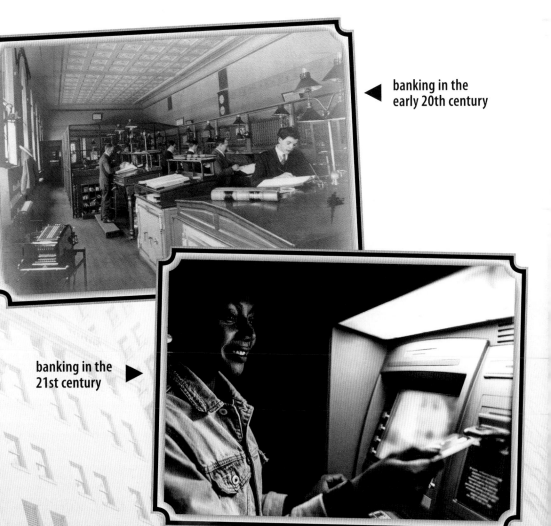

banking in the early 20th century

banking in the 21st century

Checking vs. Savings

In addition to loans, most banks also offer checking and savings accounts. People have checking accounts so that they can spend money at a moment's notice. Checking accounts are used more for spending money than saving it. People have savings accounts so that they can save money. Since they are meant to hold money, savings accounts tend to earn more interest than checking accounts do.

The government is the fourth part of the U.S. economy. It provides goods and services, but it usually doesn't sell them. Government workers provide things that almost everyone uses. They provide goods such as roads, bridges, and tunnels. This is called **infrastructure**. The government also provides services. Public schools offer a service. So do police and fire departments. Government workers also train troops for the military. All these things can serve the public good.

The U.S. government also has programs to help people in need. These programs are part of the *social safety net*. The idea is to "catch" people before they fall into serious trouble. There are many different programs in the social safety net. Retired people receive **Social Security** payments. Medicare helps elderly people pay for healthcare. Food stamps help people who can't easily afford to buy groceries.

All these goods and services are part of the U.S. economy. The government spends money to pay for these programs. It gets this money from people in households and businesses.

The Bank of the United States

The government also works with banks. The U.S. government's bank is called the Federal Reserve System. It is also called "the Fed." The Fed is in charge of keeping the economy **stable**. Workers at the Fed watch other banks and make sure people's money stays safe.

Public vs. Private

The government is also called the *public sector*. Businesses are part of the *private sector*. The two sectors can work together. For example, the government might collect money to fix roads. Government workers then use the money to hire companies to do the actual labor.

▲ first printing of food stamps

F.S.C.C.   F.S.C.C.

25 CENT
NON-TRANSFERABLE
FOOD ORDER

SUBJECT TO CONDITIONS
PRESCRIBED BY THE SECRETARY
OF AGRICULTURE

25   25

The goods and services that the government provides are paid for by taxes. People in households and businesses pay taxes. There are many different types of taxes. One type of tax is called **income tax**. With that tax, the U.S. government takes a percentage of the money that people in households and businesses make every year. Some states and cities tax income as well.

Local governments raise money through **sales taxes**. Business owners pay a small percentage of every sale they make in tax. They usually pass this cost on to customers. In this way, governments tax the clothes you wear and the movies you watch. Governments also raise money through **fines**, such as parking tickets.

Without taxes, the government wouldn't be able to provide its goods and services. The government helps in ways that businesses cannot or will not. For example, no single business has the resources to build roads for everyone to use. But people need roads. So, government workers build them, using everyone's money. In this way, taxes can be used to help the economy. However, taxes can also hurt the economy. Taxes take away money that people could otherwise spend on other things. Lawmakers have to decide the right balance.

Talking about Taxes

Income taxes are due in the United States every year, on or around April 15. This day is commonly called Tax Day. Taxes can be very complex. In fact, there are thousands of pages of federal tax laws!

This woman fills out her yearly tax forms. ▶

5.9
5.95
19.95
2.00

1: 33.85
    2.83
    36.68
6.68

12-06-05
1 *   2.19
1 *   2.19
       4.38 ST
        .37 TAX
I   4.75 CA
         2
№ 0030   1 CLK
   19-04

GUEST

Date	Table	Gues

132

YOUR RECEIPT

THANK YOU

12-28-05
01   13.00
02   5.50
03   1.50
     20.00 ST
     20.00 CA
Q   3
№ 0016   1 CLK
   13-16

Tax

Total

States without Sales Tax

Most states charge sales tax. However, five states do not. To make up for the difference, lawmakers in these five states charge higher rates for other taxes. For example, Oregon does not charge sales tax, but it has one of the highest income tax rates in the nation.

The U.S. government **regulates** businesses. *Regulations* are laws that businesses have to follow. Business owners are always trying to make profits. Laws keep them from hurting the public while trying to make money. For example, one regulation might have to deal with the environment. Factories often produce waste while making products. It can be expensive to dispose of that waste safely. It might be less expensive to put it in a nearby river. However, that could **pollute** the water that people drink. So, regulations make it illegal to dump waste in the river.

This man works for the Federal Trade Commission, which regulates businesses in the United States.

Making Things Fair

Some regulations help to keep things fair. They do this by making it illegal to steal other people's ideas. These ideas are known as intellectual property. Intellectual property laws make sure that whoever came up with an idea is the one who profits from it.

Another type of regulation meant to keep people safe affects restaurant owners. Laws require restaurant owners to keep their kitchens clean. Government workers **inspect** them to make sure they are following the law. This makes business more expensive for the restaurant owners. They have to pay for people to clean kitchens. However, it is more expensive for them not to follow the law. They can be fined for having dirty kitchens. They can even be shut down. Lawmakers have to decide how much to regulate. Too many laws can make it too hard to do business. Too few laws can lead to other problems.

Government Inspections

During health inspections, each restaurant starts off with a score of 100. Every time the health inspector sees something wrong, they subtract points. If it is something small, it might only be a few points. If it is something that could cause a health risk, then the health inspector subtracts a lot of points. At the end of the visit, restaurant owners are given a card with an A, B, or C grade, depending on their score.

POLLUTION PROHIBITED

IT IS UNLAWFUL TO DISCHARGE OR DEPOSIT INTO
OR UPON THE WATERS OF THE STATE OF MARYLAND

**OIL, GARBAGE, REFUSE OR
WASTES OF ANY KIND**

DUMPING OR DEPOSITING SUCH WASTES ON LAND
BUT IN CLOSE PROXIMITY TO STATE WATERS SO
THAT POLLUTION MAY RESULT, IS ALSO UNLAWFUL

WARNING

VIOLATORS SUBJECT TO A $500 FINE
AND IMPRISONMENT FOR 90 DAYS

STATE OF MARYLAND
DEPARTMENT OF WATER RESOURCES
ANNAPOLIS, MD.   PHONE: 268-3371

◄ Government workers post anti-pollution signs near a river in Maryland in 1965.

People in the government try not to control the economy too much. The United States is a **capitalist** country. That means people in households and businesses control the economy. They make decisions about what to make and buy. There are some rules, but most people are free to do what they want with their money. This is called *free enterprise*. The idea is that people know best how to use their money.

Sometimes, people in the government have to take a more active role in controlling the economy. This is usually during times of emergency, such as wars. In World War II, the country had to support millions of soldiers. They had to send huge amounts of food, clothing, and weapons to their soldiers. However, countries have limited resources. To make sure there were enough resources to fight the war, lawmakers decided to **ration** goods. This meant people could only buy a certain amount of important items. The rest went to the war effort. Rubber, gas, meat, and sugar were all rationed. This type of government control is rare.

Opportunity Costs

During the war, people knew they could help the war effort by rationing goods, but that meant they would have to give up other things they wanted. This type of decision is known as an *opportunity cost*. The *cost* is what you give up. For example, during the war, people wanted to buy food whenever they wanted. They also wanted the United States to win the war. People rationed to help win the war. The opportunity cost was the extra food they had to give up.

SAVE
SIMPLIFY
SUBSTITUTE

A woman reads about wartime rationing in 1942. ▶

In 1943, Americans stand in line to get ration books, which will tell them how much of certain goods they can buy.

SHOES

RATIONING BOARD

WAR BOOK 2   WAR BOOK I

RATIONING BOARD
GASOLINE   TIRES

The Flow of Resources

People in households consume goods and services produced by businesses. They choose what to buy and how much. Their choices create demand for different goods and services. Businesses fulfill the demands of **consumers** by producing the things they want and need. Think of the baker making peach pies. They know that people will want pies. They are meeting people's demands. If the customers' tastes change, the baker will have to change to meet their new demands.

Resources flow back and forth between people in households and businesses. Here's one way to think about it: The bakery worker sells their labor making peach pies. In return, they earn a paycheck. They can use that money to buy things they want. They can also spend it on something else, such as an airline ticket. The money the airline makes eventually goes back to someone who lives in a household. That person might use it to buy peach pies. This is how household consumers drive the economy.

Where the Money Goes

The average American adult spends most of their money on housing. This includes rent or payments on home loans. Transportation is the second-biggest expense, and food is the third.

ECONOMY FLOW

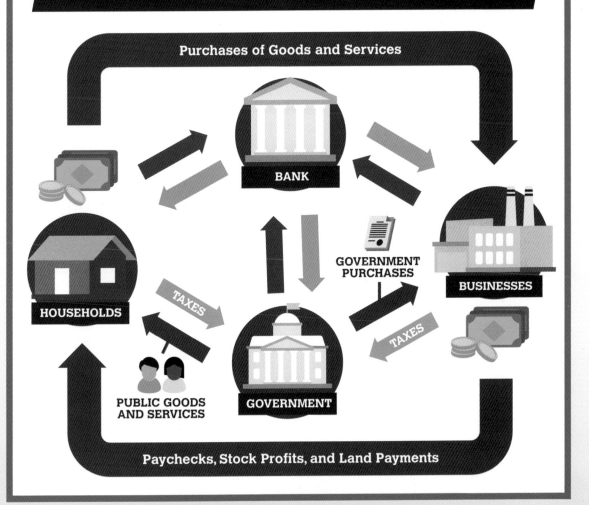

Purchases of Goods and Services

BANK

GOVERNMENT PURCHASES

BUSINESSES

HOUSEHOLDS

TAXES

TAXES

PUBLIC GOODS AND SERVICES

GOVERNMENT

Paychecks, Stock Profits, and Land Payments

Supply and Demand

Economies run on a system of supply and demand. When demand goes up, usually supply goes up. For example, imagine a movie that is based on a book comes to theaters. Crowds love the movie, so the demand for the book goes up. The book's publisher has to meet that demand, so it prints more books. Once demand goes down, the publisher can supply fewer books.

The exchange of resources is called *trade*. Both parties benefit from this exchange. Buyers get something they want. The seller receives money for that good or service. These interactions are what make the economy work.

Trade helps the economy grow. That's because trade creates more trade. When business owners sell things, they have more money. They can buy land, labor, and capital from households. People in those households then have more money. They can buy goods and services from businesses. Or, they can put their money in bank accounts for bankers to loan other people. Entrepreneurs can also use that money to start new businesses.

When there is less trade, the economy shrinks. Businesses sell fewer things. Companies cannot afford to pay for labor, so people lose their jobs. People in households make less money and cannot afford to buy things. Demand for goods and services drops.

To help with these problems, countries try to encourage trade. In the early twentieth century, the U.S. government did just that. It built a **canal** through Panama to increase trade with Europe and Africa. The Panama Canal worked! Trade increased, and the economy grew.

Lock It Down

The Panama Canal uses a series of "locks" to move ships back and forth from the Atlantic to the Pacific Oceans. Locks are sections of water that are bordered by gates. To raise ships, more water is added between the gates. To lower ships, water is removed from between gates. Locks like those in the Panama Canal help ships cross land easier.

Panama Canal

The Panama Canal connects the Pacific and Atlantic Oceans. When it opened in 1914, it changed the way the world traded goods. Ships no longer had to sail around the southern tip of South America. Businesses could move things faster and easier. This made their products cheaper to buy, so consumers bought more of them.

construction of the
Panama Canal in 1913 ▲

PACIFIC   PANAMA   OCEAN

Cruces

Gorgona

COLON
(Aspinwall)

ATLANTIC   OCEAN

Chagres

PANORAMIC VIEW
OF THE
CANAL OF PANAMA

From the relief constructed by Cn. Meurt on official documents.

Making Tough Decisions

The United States economy is enormous and complex. There are many moving parts, and they all have to come together for the economy to succeed. Regardless of how large it is, everyone plays a role in the economy. People in households, businesses, banks, and the government have to work together. They all contribute to one another's successes and failures.

You interact with all four sectors of the economy on a daily basis. People in your household buy things from businesses. Workers in your household sell things too. Every time they go to work, they are selling their labor for money. Anytime you put money in the bank or use a debit card for a purchase, you are interacting with the banking sector. The public goods and services you use come from the government. Every day, people rely on all four sectors to live their lives. The sectors must work together for the economy to thrive.

Everyone faces decisions. *Should I buy this? Should I save money for the future?* The decisions you make have a big impact. Take time to weigh your options. After all, the choices you make will affect the future of the nation's economy.

Free Market

Every year, countries are ranked on how free their economies are. The freest economies are the ones that have the least government influence and the fewest regulations. In 2019, the United States was ranked number 12. That means there are only 11 countries in the world that have freer economies. The freest economy was Hong Kong. The least free economy was North Korea.

Growth Rates

People measure economies in many ways. One way is to measure the value of everything that a country produces in a year. Then, those totals can be compared to other years. This comparison shows whether a country's economy is growing or shrinking. Over the past decade, the U.S. economy has grown by about two percent each year.

COUNTY OF LOS ANGELES
Public Health
Environmental Health

FOOD FACILITY SELF-INSPECTION CHECKLIST

The Self-Inspection Checklist is provided as a guideline for the food operator to use in evaluating their facility's operation and food handling practices. It is separated into High Risk Factors and Low Risk Factors that are based on the same food safety principles as the Food Official Inspection Report (FOIR) or Compliance Report.

Note: Although the safety principles used on this Self-Inspection Guide are the same as used on the FOIR, the order of the categories on this form does not necessarily follow the same order used on the FOIR.

	MET	NOT MET
HIGH RISK FACTORS		
EMPLOYEE HEALTH, HYGIENE & PRACTICES		
1. At least one (1) employee is a Certified Food Protection Manager. Certificate is valid and available at the site.		
2. All employees handling food (including preparation and service) and utensils must have a valid Food Handler Card. Certificate or copy available at the site.		
3. Employees have food safety knowledge that is related to their assigned duties (i.e., cooking, cooling, warewashing, etc.)		
4. Employees appear in good health. No reports of illness or food employees are not experiencing persistent sneezing, coughing, or runny nose that is connected with discharges from their eyes, nose, or mouth.		
5. Employees have no open sores, cuts, on hands or fingers.		
6. Employee wears clean outer clothing / apron.		
7. Hair of employees is properly confined (i.e., hairnets, caps, etc.)		
8. Food employees fingernails are trimmed, filed, and clean.		
9. Employees do not eat, drink, chew gum and smoke in utensil washing/storage areas; food preparation and storage areas.		
10. Food employee drinks from a closed beverage container and stored correctly to prevent contamination.		
11. Clothing and personal belongings are stored away from food.		
12. Food employees will not care for or handle animals that are allowed in the food facility, such as service or patrol animals.		
13. A person in charge (PIC) is present and performs his/her duties during all hours of operation.		
PROPER HANDWASHING, SUPPLIES AND PROPER USE OF GLOVES		
14. Employees wash their hands with soap and warm water (100°F) for 15 seconds for the following reasons: a) before starting work, b) immediately after using the restrooms, c) after handling raw animal products or unwashed produce, d) when there is hand contact with hair, skin, and clothes, e) any time needed to prevent food contamination.		
15. *Employees wash their hands only in approved hand wash sinks.*		
16. Hand sinks are accessible for use.		
17. Single use towels and soap at dispensers are available.		

Regulate It!

One of the most important regulations in the United States is the mandatory inspections of all food-service establishments. Different counties have different food-inspection rules. An example of these rules might be:

- Major violations (such as a sick worker handling food) will result in a 4-point subtraction.

- Minor violations (such as a worker who sneezes but is not sick) will result in a 2-point subtraction.

- Good practices violations (such as a customer being allowed too close to the food preparation area) will result in a 1-point subtraction.

Imagine you are in charge of creating food-inspection rules. Create a list of five violations in each category—Major, Minor, and Good Practices—that you think all restaurants should follow. Decide how many points should be subtracted for each violation. Then, compare your list with friends to see what practices they think are important.

Glossary

canal—a passage for boats

capitalist—a system in which goods and production are privately owned

consumers—people who buy and use goods

demand—a desire and ability to buy goods or services at a certain time and price

efficient—able to produce the desired results without wasting time, energy, or materials

entrepreneurship—the act of taking on financial risks to make a profit

fines—amounts of money to be paid as punishment

income tax—money taken from a person's or business's profits

infrastructure—a system of basic structures and facilities

inspect—examine closely for quality or condition

invest—use money to purchase stock, property, or other things in order to make more money

loans—money that is lent to people to be paid back

pollute—make impure or spoil with waste

profits—money that is made after all expenses have been taken out

ration—use things carefully so as not to use too much

regulates—governs according to rules and laws

retirement—the act of ending one's working or professional career

salary—money paid at regular times for services or work provided

sales taxes—money paid on the purchases of goods and services

sectors—parts

Social Security—a U.S. government program that gives money to retired, unemployed, and disabled people

stable—not likely to change or not easily changed

stock exchanges—places where people buy and sell ownership in certain companies

Index

Your Turn!

The United States has one of the largest economies in the world. However, more and more Americans are buying goods from other countries. This is great for the world economy, but it can negatively affect the U.S. economy.

Research the pros and cons of buying goods from the United States and buying goods from foreign countries. Create a Venn diagram to display your research. Compare and contrast buying American goods versus buying foreign goods. Then, pick a side. Try to follow through with the side you choose in your buying decisions.